A Lovesome Thing

A Play

Jean McConnell

FOR AMATEUR PRODUCTION ENQUIRIES

UNITED KINGDOM AND WORLD
EXCLUDING NORTH AMERICA
plays@SamuelFrench-London.co.uk
020 7255 4302/01

Each title is subject to availability from Samuel French,

depending upon country of performance.

CHARACTERS

<table>
<tr><td>Mrs Baxter</td><td rowspan="4">}</td><td rowspan="3">Members of the Little
Dowgate Branch of the
Women's Institute</td></tr>
<tr><td>Mrs Wells</td></tr>
<tr><td>Mrs Fairbrother</td></tr>
<tr><td>Mrs Festoon</td></tr>
</table>

Lady Cleveland, of Dowgate Hall
Elsie, Lady Cleveland's housekeeper
Miss Hodge, neighbour
Mrs Willis, neighbour

The action takes place in the conservatory of Dowgate Hall

A LOVESOME THING

The conservatory of Dowgate Hall

It is an elegant place, with plants set amongst the garden furniture. An entrance UR *leads into the house, and below it is a settee.* UC *is a table with a chair beside it. An entrance* L *leads into the garden.* DL *is a chair with a small table below it.* DC *is a low table. On it stands a broken pot plant*

Mrs Baxter is endeavouring to support the broken plant. Like the other W.I. ladies, she is dressed in gardening clothes. Each time she lets go of the plant, it falls over. At last, she calls towards the garden

Mrs Baxter Mrs Wells! Mrs Wells!
Mrs Wells (*off*, L) What is it, Mrs Baxter?
Mrs Baxter Come here quickly!
Mrs Wells I can't come. I'm in the middle of something. What do you want?
Mrs Baxter What does it matter what I want if you aren't coming? (*She calls*) Mrs Fairbrother!
Mrs Fairbrother (*off*, L) Yes, Mrs Baxter?
Mrs Baxter Will you come here a minute!
Mrs Fairbrother Why?
Mrs Baxter Oh, really! (*She calls*) I've broken one of Lady Cleveland's plants—that's why!

Mrs Fairbrother, carrying a garden fork, and Mrs Wells, with a pair of clippers, enter L, *hurrying. They converge on the broken plant*

Mrs Fairbrother Oh, what a shame.
Mrs Wells I had one of those. They cost ever so much.
Mrs Fairbrother I can't imagine what you were doing.
Mrs Wells Ever so expensive. Come from abroad.
Mrs Fairbrother A lovely specimen. I was only saying the other day…
Mrs Baxter Don't fuss. Don't fuss. I can fix it if you'll just get me a little stake.
Mrs Fairbrother Steak?
Mrs Wells I hope you're right.
Mrs Fairbrother Lady Cleveland's beautiful plant.
Mrs Baxter Lady Cleveland will never even know.
Mrs Wells Elsie will.

Elsie enters R

Mrs Baxter We'll just have to keep it from Elsie. After all, it isn't Elsie's plant——

The others point at Elsie

——and it's none of Elsie's business if—— (*She becomes aware of their pointing*) Oh, hallo, Elsie.
Elsie What have you done to madam's plant?
Mrs Baxter It was a pure accident. I just happened to brush against it, and it went flying.

Lady Cleveland enters R

Elsie Brushed against it indeed. Clumsy great… (*She sees Lady*

Cleveland) Here, madam, look at your nice plant. (*She brings it to her,* R)

Lady Cleveland That will do, Elsie.

Mrs Fairbrother Come now, Elsie. Mrs Baxter couldn't help it.

Mrs Wells Come to that, it would have been dead already if we hadn't been watering it.

Elsie It wasn't supposed to be watered all that much.

Elsie takes the plant, exits, and re-enters with a brush and pan

Mrs Baxter Now, Elsie, we're the gardeners here, aren't we, Lady Cleveland?

Lady Cleveland Well—yes—and it's most kind of you—but I really don't like you putting yourselves out in this way.

The three ladies converge on Lady Cleveland

Mrs Baxter Nonsense! Many's the helping hand you've given our organisation in the past. You've contributed to our funds, sent us jumble, let us hold fêtes in your grounds. I said to our members, "Here's our chance to repay some of this kindness. We can't allow Lady Cleveland's lovely garden to go to ruin for want of a helping hand."

Mrs Fairbrother Old Bates always keeps it so beautifully.

Lady Cleveland Yes. He's a rare treasure.

Mrs Wells Poor old Bates.

Mrs Baxter He'll be so glad we're keeping the garden up while he's in hospital. Stop him worrying about it.

Elsie (*tidying up* DC) I doubt that.

Mrs Baxter Help him get better quicker.

Elsie You're right there!

Elsie wrests the garden fork from Mrs Fairbrother and exits L

Mrs Baxter Mrs Fairbrother, have you dug over the herbaceous border?

Mrs Fairbrother Well—I'm getting on. There's an awful lot of it.

Mrs Baxter I'm not criticising. I was just thinking, autumn is the time for replanting, you know. (*She moves* DC *and makes notes at the low table*)

The other two ladies join her

Elsie enters L *and moves up stage*

Lady Cleveland Don't you think we ought to leave that for when Bates comes back?

Mrs Baxter No times like the present. Get things established before the winter. I thought we might give over the little walled part to shrubs—they're so labour-saving.

Lady Cleveland But that's the Elizabethan knot garden.

Mrs Baxter Quite. Needs planting up.

Lady Cleveland Er—we are in the National Garden Scheme. Open to the public. Bates is very proud.

Mrs Baxter Oh, with reason, Lady Cleveland. But if you let Nature get its way...

Lady Cleveland (*defeated*) Just a little tidying up, perhaps.

Mrs Baxter Mrs Wells, take Lady Cleveland down the path and show her the hedge you've clipped.

Mrs Wells (*moving towards exit* L) I've not done it before, you know. But I think I've got a real flair...

Lady Cleveland and Mrs Wells exit L

Mrs Baxter It's going to look simply lovely again.

Mrs Fairbrother It will. It will.

Mrs Baxter You aim for colour in all seasons, you know.

Mrs Fairbrother A garden is a lovesome thing, God wot.

Elsie and Mrs Baxter stare at her

Mrs Baxter What did you say?
Mrs Fairbrother I just read it on a calendar.
Mrs Baxter Oh. The weeds are our worst enemy, of course. They've quite won the day in some areas. I intend to mount a special campaign.

Mrs Baxter sits DL, *making notes. Elsie tidies* DR. *Mrs Fairbrother hovers between the two*

Mrs Fairbrother There are a dreadful lot.
Mrs Baxter Drastic measures are called for.
Elsie What about a flame thrower?
Mrs Fairbrother Oh, no, please!
Mrs Baxter Elsie was only joking, Mrs Fairbrother. I'll have you know, Elsie, there are any number of effective weedkillers.
Elsie I know. Tasteless too, Mrs Fairbrother.
Mrs Fairbrother Oh, you will be careful, won't you?
Mrs Baxter We've a tough job on hand. No good being squeamish. (*She rises*) We've come here to battle with Nature. We must take the bull by the horns. That reminds me; we should get hold of some rich farmyard manure.
Mrs Fairbrother Well, please don't look at *me!*
Mrs Baxter We can probably get it delivered.
Elsie There are horses over in the stable block.
Mrs Baxter Just the thing, Elsie. Mrs Fairbrother, you can take a wheelbarrow over and shovel and——
Mrs Fairbrother I think I'm going to be ill!
Mrs Baxter Oh, very well, I'll do it. Tch!

Lady Cleveland and Mrs Wells enter L

Ah. Did you see the good work?

Lady Cleveland (*crossing to* R, *coughing weakly*) Not very well, there's so much smoke out there.

Lady Cleveland leans on Elsie for support

Mrs Baxter That's my bonfire. Isn't it grand? I'll just go and stoke it up.

Mrs Wells It seems quite big already, Mrs Baxter. Do you think it's wise?

Mrs Baxter Nonsense. Must keep it going.

Mrs Baxter exits L

Mrs Wells shrugs and moves R. *Mrs Fairbrother, Elsie and Lady Cleveland move to look out into the garden* L

Mrs Fairbrother How is it getting on?

Elsie Like a house on fire—which it will be if she doesn't watch out.

Lady Cleveland She has built it up a bit. (*She calls*) I shouldn't put any more on, Mrs Baxter. Mrs Baxter! Oh, good, she's coming back.

Elsie Bates always has his bonfires down beyond the orchard.

Lady Cleveland So he does.

Elsie She'll be setting the pergola alight next.

Lady Cleveland Oh, no!

Mrs Baxter enters L

Mrs Baxter Don't worry. It's just a little green, that's all. Is there any paraffin?

Lady Cleveland } (*together*) No!
Elsie

Mrs Wells
Mrs Fairbrother } (*together*) Yes. I saw a can in the shed.
Mrs Baxter Come along, then, Mrs Fairbrother. Bring me the can of paraffin. Come along.

Mrs Baxter exits L

Mrs Fairbrother (*following her*) Paraffin. Yes, Mrs Baxter.

Mrs Fairbrother exits L

Elsie A bit green, she says. What a smother.
Mrs Wells It'll make a wonderful clearance though.
Lady Cleveland (*peering off* L) I can't even see them now. Where have they got to?
Mrs Wells They're in the smoke somewhere.
Lady Cleveland I thought they'd gone.
Elsie No such luck.
Mrs Wells I don't think you appreciate Mrs Baxter's true qualities, Elsie. We're very fortunate to have such an organiser. She is a *leader*.
Elsie So was Hitler.
Lady Cleveland (*calling*) Mrs Baxter, don't put any more paraffin on! Mrs Baxter, mind how you go. *Mrs Baxter!*

Mrs Fairbrother screams off stage

Mrs Wells Oh, good heavens!
Elsie Now she's done it.
Lady Cleveland I hope that overhanging branch won't catch fire.

Mrs Baxter enters L, *cheerfully*

Mrs Baxter There! That's got it going. Marvellous what a spot of paraffin will do. Oh, have you got a little butter, Elsie?
Elsie Butter?
Mrs Baxter Yes, Mrs Fairbrother was standing a bit close.

Mrs Fairbrother enters L, *moaning and clutching her hand*

Lady Cleveland, Mrs Wells and Elsie hurry to support her

Lady Cleveland Are you all right?
Mrs Baxter (*moving* R) Course she is. It's only superficial. Bit silly, wasn't it, stepping in like that?
Mrs Fairbrother You might have said what you were going to do!
Mrs Baxter Never mind. It's nothing much.
Mrs Wells Does it hurt, love?
Mrs Baxter Where's the butter?
Mrs Wells It's baking powder you should use.
Mrs Baxter Rubbish—butter's the stuff.
Elsie You're not making a cake. There's some ointment in the bathroom especially for burns.
Lady Cleveland So there is. Do come with me, Mrs Fairbrother. I knew it would come in handy one day.

Lady Cleveland leads Mrs Fairbrother and they exit R

Mrs Wells (*moving to Mrs Baxter,* R) Poor Mrs Fairbrother. She turned quite white.
Mrs Baxter Mrs Fairbrother's accident prone; we're certainly discovering that.

Miss Hodge enters L. *She is very cross*

Miss Hodge Ah, there you are!

Elsie Oh, hallo, Miss Hodge. (*To the others*) This is Miss Hodge from the stable block.

Mrs Wells
Mrs Baxter } (*together*) How do you do...

Miss Hodge Are you going on much longer making this smoke everywhere?

Mrs Baxter I—er—is it blowing over your way?

Miss Hodge Right in my window!

Mrs Baxter I'm terribly sorry, I'd no idea.

Miss Hodge All over the yard. The ponies are getting extremely restive.

Mrs Baxter Nasty for you. Yes, I'm so sorry.

Miss Hodge What are you going to do about it?

Mrs Baxter Well, actually, I've only just lit it and——

Miss Hodge It's not very civil, you know, day after day.

Mrs Baxter No. No. I'll put it out of course——

Miss Hodge That's right.

Mrs Baxter Quite soon.

Miss Hodge You'll put it out now! Pronto! Or I may telephone the Minister of the Environment.

Mrs Baxter
Mrs Wells } (*exchanging looks; together*) Minister of the Environment?

Miss Hodge He happens to be a distant cousin.

Mrs Wells
Mrs Baxter } (*together*) { Oh.
{ Oh. We'll put it out straight away.

Mrs Wells We will. We will.

Miss Hodge Don't say you weren't warned. (*She moves* L) Disgraceful!

Miss Hodge exits

Elsie Miserable old——

Mrs Baxter (*interrupting*) No, Elsie, the woman's entitled to speak. You don't want to argue. (*She turns to Mrs Wells*) Never argue. Just agree politely, then go on doing what you want to.

Mrs Baxter and Mrs Wells chuckle

Mrs Willis enters L

Mrs Willis Are you Lady Cleveland's gardeners?
Mrs Baxter Sort of. While poor Bates is away, you know.
Mrs Willis Well, if you don't put out that bonfire, you can come and do all my washing again.
Elsie Is it blowing into your cottage, Mrs Willis?
Mrs Willis Lumps of soot coming down like a volcanic eruption.
Mrs Baxter Oh, I think you're exaggerating.
Mrs Willis And the smell! Like a funeral pyre on the Ganges.
Mrs Wells That's not very nice.
Mrs Baxter I'm sorry if it's causing inconvenience.
Mrs Willis Inconvenience? If you don't see to it, I'll call the police. (*She moves to exit* L) Call yourself gardeners! Old Bates would turn in his grave!
Mrs Baxter He's not dead.
Mrs Willis Even so!

Mrs Willis exits L

Mrs Wells How rude.
Mrs Baxter (*sighing*) Mrs Wells, come and help me shovel some earth on that fire, will you?

Mrs Baxter and Mrs Wells exit L

Lady Cleveland enters R

Lady Cleveland (*moving to Elsie,* C) Mrs Fairbrother is taking an aspirin.

Elsie If you don't mind my saying so, madam, I think it's a great mistake letting this lot loose in our nice garden.

Lady Cleveland They're doing their best.

Elsie Pulled up the lily of the valley.

Lady Cleveland That was a mistake.

Elsie Cutting down the magnolia.

Lady Cleveland They thought it was dead.

Elsie And what about the sundial?

Lady Cleveland It *was* a pity about the sundial.

Elsie You shouldn't have given them their head with the motor-mower. In fact, if you ask me, you shouldn't have given them their head at all.

Lady Cleveland How could I refuse when they meant it so kindly? And they're working so very hard. And Bates should be back very soon now.

Elsie How soon, madam?

Lady Cleveland Any time, I believe. It was only a grumbling appendix, after all, apparently.

Elsie It's not only his appendix will be grumbling when he sees this lot.

Lady Cleveland Oh, don't, Elsie. They're so enthusiastic. One hates to discourage them.

Elsie I don't. You're too good-hearted, madam. Well, let's hope Bates comes back before they've wrecked the ground completely.

Lady Cleveland Oh, they won't do that, Elsie. At least… Let's give them another tea break!

Mrs Fairbrother enters R

Feeling better, Mrs Fairbrother?

Mrs Fairbrother Yes, thank you.

Lady Cleveland Come along, Elsie. (*She moves to exit* R)

Elsie (*following her*) The swiss roll, madam?

Lady Cleveland Yes. Call the others, will you, Mrs Fairbrother?

Lady Cleveland and Elsie exit R

Mrs Fairbrother Mrs Wells! Mrs Baxter! Yoo-hoo! (*She sits down* R, *nursing her hand*)
Mrs Baxter (*off*) Shoo! Shoo!

Mrs Baxter enters L

Those blessed birds!

Mrs Wells enters L

Mrs Wells Wretched birds! They've been here all day. You'd think they were half-starved. (*She sits down*, DL)
Mrs Fairbrother That special seed must be very tasty. It's the second lot I've planted, you know.
Mrs Baxter It is rather discouraging.
Mrs Fairbrother Perhaps we ought to accept defeat.
Mrs Baxter No! We can't let Lady Cleveland down. We said we'd re-grass that section of lawn that got in the way of the rotovator. (*She glances off*, L) Oh, would you believe it! There's another flock! (*She shakes her fist*) Hi! Hi! Hi!

Elsie enters L. *She carries a tea tray*

Elsie What's the matter with old green fingers?
Mrs Baxter (*shouting off*, L) I'll come and wring your neck in a minute!
Elsie Anyone we know? (*She sets the tray on the table* UC)
Mrs Wells It's those starlings. They must tell each other.
Elsie Perhaps you should have concreted the whole lot over.

Mrs Baxter It makes you appreciate why farmers are always so sour. But we mustn't let it get us down.
Elsie I suggest a scarecrow.
Mrs Baxter Well, why don't you comb your hair?
Elsie Oh ha-ha-ha.
Mrs Wells No, seriously, Mrs Baxter, isn't that a good idea? We could dress up a broom in some old clothes.
Mrs Baxter Look, if they don't care a hoot when we're standing there in the flesh, they're going to laugh themselves silly at a scarecrow.
Mrs Wells I think it's worth a try.
Mrs Baxter Very well. We'll try. Have you an old broom, Elsie?
Elsie I expect so. (*She moves to exit* R) One day I'll be the ideas-man and somebody else will be the leg-man.

Elsie exits R

Mrs Baxter I wonder if Lady Cleveland has a few cast-offs?
Mrs Fairbrother No need, I have some of my husband's discarded togs in my basket. I was taking them down to Oxfam.

Mrs Fairbrother exits R

Mrs Wells Perhaps we could put out a bird table.
Mrs Baxter (*moving to her*) Pardon?
Mrs Wells I put out some cake crumbs the other day and——
Mrs Baxter You put out some crumbs?
Mrs Wells I thought it might take their minds off——
Mrs Baxter Mrs Wells, whose side are you on?
Mrs Wells I just thought.
Mrs Baxter Crumbs left out overnight attract rats.
Mrs Wells But they weren't, I just said, they ate them all up.
Mrs Baxter That's right. Build up their strength. Really!

Mrs Wells I just thought...

Mrs Baxter I do wish you'd stop thinking, Mrs Wells. Please! Leave the thinking to me. Now, what are you going to do in future?

Mrs Wells Leave the thinking to you.

Mrs Baxter Right. (*She moves* R, *takes out her notebook and sits*) Now then, let's check the list. Ah yes, the rose bushes.

Mrs Wells You mean the ones we were going to replace because you——

Mrs Baxter Yes, yes, yes. Six, I think, we said.

Mrs Wells Six, that's right.

Mrs Baxter You did take the order to the nurseryman, Mrs Wells?

Mrs Wells I certainly did. Haven't they turned up?

Mrs Baxter No, they haven't.

Mrs Wells I wrote them down just as you said, and I took it down on last Tuesday. Or was it Wednesday?

Mrs Baxter I hope you got it right. (*She checks her notes*) Two Peace, one Shot Silk, two Ena Harkness and...

Mrs Wells And one Cabbage White.

Mrs Baxter One Cabbage... No, no, no. There's no such rose as a Cabbage White.

Mrs Wells What do you mean? Everyone's heard of a Cabbage White.

Mrs Baxter Very likely, but it isn't a rose. Definitely. Good heavens, Mrs Wells.

Mrs Wells What is it then?

Mrs Baxter For goodness sake, my dear woman—a cabbage.

Mrs Wells But... (*She thinks better of it and stops*)

Elsie and Mrs Fairbrother enter R. *They carry a scarecrow*

Mrs Baxter (*rising*) Ah!

Elsie Hold it steady, Mrs Fairbrother. There!

Mrs Fairbrother There! What do you think?
Mrs Baxter Oh, just look! Mr Fairbrother to the life!

Everyone laughs, except Mrs Fairbrother

Mrs Fairbrother He happens to be a very fine man.
Mrs Baxter Now, don't take offence.
Mrs Fairbrother A very good man.
Mrs Baxter It was only a joke.
Mrs Fairbrother No-one ever had a better husband.
Mrs Baxter Of course not, Mrs Fairbrother.
Mrs Fairbrother And he could teach you a thing or two about
   gardening, so there!
Elsie He'll be just the chap to put up then, won't he?
Mrs Baxter Elsie!
Elsie Why don't you try him out?
Mrs Baxter Why don't you shut up! Let's get it down the garden,
   Mrs Wells.

Mrs Baxter and Mrs Wells take the scarecrow and exit L

Elsie (*calling after them*) Your tea's just coming up.
Mrs Fairbrother That was very hurtful. (*She sits* R)
Elsie They didn't mean it, I'm sure.
Mrs Fairbrother Don't you think so? Mr Fairbrother *is* rather
   thin.
Elsie Never in your life.

Mrs Fairbrother is mollified

Lady Cleveland enters R, *with a teapot*

Lady Cleveland The tea's ready, Elsie. Where are the others?
Elsie (*taking the pot*) In the garden, madam.

Lady Cleveland Oh yes. (*She calls off*, L) Teatime, Mrs Baxter! Mrs Wells! Oh, and do ask Mr Fairbrother to join us, I didn't know he was here.

Mrs Fairbrother bursts into tears

Elsie (*comforting her*) Lady Cleveland hasn't got her glasses on. Truly.
Lady Cleveland What's the matter, Mrs Fairbrother? Burn painful? Do have some tea. Elsie, hurry.
Elsie Yes, madam.

Lady Cleveland serves the tea. Elsie assists her

Mrs Baxter and Mrs Wells enter L

Mrs Wells sits down L

Lady Cleveland Now, is this all of you or are there any more down in the shrubbery?
Mrs Wells Just us. Mrs Festoon didn't turn up.
Mrs Baxter She *knew* she was on the roster for today too.
Lady Cleveland Never mind. You've done splendidly. Why not call it a day?
Mrs Baxter Oh, we've lots to do yet. There's Mrs Wells's topiary...
Lady Cleveland Oh.
Mrs Wells I've only clipped one side so far, but I'll soon have it back to a lovely peacock again.
Elsie But it used to be a bear.
Lady Cleveland Never mind, Elsie.
Mrs Baxter We've put up a scarecrow, Lady Cleveland, did you see? I think it's going to be very effective. The starlings are the trouble. There's one particular one. A great, big, greedy bird. Just waits for me to turn my back, and then... (*She glances* L)

Dear life! He's there again! (*She moves to the entrance* L)
Mrs Fairbrother Oh, no!

Mrs Wells and Mrs Fairbrother join Mrs Baxter

Mrs Baxter (*shouting*) Get off, you thieving, wicked vulture!
Mrs Wells Shoo! Get along!
Mrs Fairbrother Be off with you! Horrid thing!
Mrs Baxter I've had enough. Give me something… (*She grabs a trowel from nearby*) I'll fix him.
Lady Cleveland Mrs Baxter, please!
Mrs Baxter (*hurling the trowel off stage* L) Gar! Take that! Ooops, sorry.
Mrs Wells Mrs Baxter, you've hit it!
Mrs Fairbrother Oh, dear—you've hit it!
Elsie You've hit the little perisher.
Mrs Baxter Oh Lord!
Lady Cleveland (*joining the group*) Well, fancy doing that.
Mrs Fairbrother You've killed it!
Mrs Baxter I didn't mean to.
Mrs Wells Well, don't just stand there. Go and get it.

Mrs Baxter exits L *in a hurry*

Mrs Fairbrother Poor little mite. There's a society for the protection of birds, you know.
Mrs Wells I should think it's finished.
Lady Cleveland No, I think I can see it trembling. We must find something to put it in. Get a box, Elsie.

Elsie exits R

Mrs Fairbrother I can't bear cruelty to animals. That's why this world's in the state it is. Battery hens. Sweated pigs!

Mrs Baxter enters L. *She carries a bird*

We'll pay for our ill-treatment of dumb creatures.
Mrs Baxter All right. All right. It's just its wing, I think.

Elsie enters R *with a box*

Mrs Wells Whatever did you do it for?
Mrs Baxter I only meant to scare it.
Elsie You've scared it all right—it's dead.

Mrs Baxter puts the bird in the box

Mrs Baxter No, no, it's only fainted.
Mrs Fairbrother Hunting and bullfighting. Someday the animal kingdom will take its revenge.
Mrs Wells Just look at it.
Mrs Baxter Well, I'm sorry. I wouldn't hurt it intentionally.
Mrs Wells What are we going to do with it?
Mrs Fairbrother We must look after it until it gets better.
Elsie If it does.
Lady Cleveland Elsie!
Mrs Fairbrother You ought to get a vet.
Mrs Baxter I don't think it's too bad. Turn it over.
Mrs Fairbrother You can do more harm by ignorance.
Mrs Baxter There! It's moved!

There is a joyous reaction all round

Mrs Fairbrother They always rally before the end.
Lady Cleveland Let's give it a chance to revive.
Mrs Baxter There! It moved again!

There is another happy reaction all round

Mrs Fairbrother Do you think it will live in captivity?
Mrs Baxter Of course it will. Be hopping around in no time.
Mrs Fairbrother Oh, how sweet. What shall we call it?
Elsie Ena Harkness.
Mrs Wells It's definitely coming round.
Mrs Baxter I told you.
Mrs Fairbrother Little love. Sweet! Sweet! Are you a hungry
    pet?
Mrs Wells Did you see that? It winked!
Mrs Fairbrother What shall we give it to eat?
Elsie Try it with a little lawn seed.

Doorbell rings

Elsie exits R

Lady Cleveland I should leave it quietly alone.
Mrs Baxter I'll put it over here. (*She puts the box* L)
Lady Cleveland What about some tea?
Mrs Fairbrother Do you think it would take it?
Lady Cleveland For *you*, Mrs Fairbrother.
Mrs Fairbrother Oh, thank you. (*She takes her cup and sits* DR)

*Elsie and Mrs Festoon enter. Mrs Festoon is carrying a
package*

Mrs Festoon Better late than never, eh?
Mrs Baxter We began at two-thirty, Mrs Festoon.
Mrs Festoon I know, but wait till you see what I've got for you.
    It's for the patch we've seeded.
Mrs Wells Don't mention that.

*Mrs Festoon puts the package on the low table down stage, and
takes from it a strange contraption with a long lead and plug*

Lady Cleveland (*apprehensively*) What is it, Mrs Festoon?
Mrs Festoon The answer to our prayers. A bird-scarer.
Elsie Not before time. They're moving in.
Mrs Festoon It goes off with a bang every hour.
Mrs Baxter What a wonderful idea!
Lady Cleveland (*faintly*) But the neighbours...
Mrs Festoon Ah, this is a special one. A sort of quiet bang. My husband got a friend to make it up in his machine shop.
Mrs Wells However did he make it, Mrs Festoon?
Mrs Festoon Well, he got a metal base, stamped, cut and spindle-drilled, attached a calibrated decimal-hour marstochron mechanism with a vibro-sensitised detonator connected to part of a stereo-chrono-cyclegraph. And then he wired the circuit for control by photo-electron rays.

A stunned silence

Mrs Baxter Splendid! Isn't that splendid, Lady Cleveland?
Lady Cleveland Oh, splendid. Excuse me, it's time for my pills.

Lady Cleveland exits R

Mrs Wells Isn't that clever, Mrs Fairbrother?
Mrs Fairbrother Oh, very clever.
Mrs Baxter Really clever, Mrs Festoon.
Mrs Festoon Thank you, Mrs Baxter. Here's the bill.

Mrs Festoon hands the bill to Mrs Baxter and goes on unpacking the bird-scarer

Mrs Baxter The bill? (*She moves* L *and gasps*)

Mrs Wells and Mrs Fairbrother look at the bill over her shoulder and gasp

Elsie looks at it, gasps, and exits R

Mrs Festoon (*after a pause*) I'll set it up for you. Now you hold
   the lead with the plug, Mrs Baxter.
Mrs Baxter Oh, thank you.
Mrs Festoon And I'll take the machine into the garden.

*Mrs Festoon hands the plug to Mrs Baxter, trails the lead from
Mrs Wells to Mrs Fairbrother, then exits* L

Mrs Baxter (*staring at the bill*) Oh, dear.
Mrs Wells I can't afford it and that's that.
Mrs Fairbrother It is rather steep.
Mrs Baxter But she's made it now.
Mrs Wells She should have asked us first.
Mrs Fairbrother I thought she was giving it to us.
Mrs Baxter Well, she's not, is she?
Mrs Wells It's too much, and I'm not paying. You're not to pay,
   Mrs Fairbrother.
Mrs Baxter But she's out there fixing it up. And it's not as if she
   can sell it elsewhere. Not many people want a bird-scarer.
Mrs Wells Not at that price, they don't.
Mrs Festoon (*off*) Plug it in, please!
Mrs Baxter (*calling*) Yes, Mrs Festoon! (*To others*) Where's the
   power point?

They move about looking for the power point, without success

   You know, if we shared the cost between the whole garden
   roster...
Mrs Wells It's the principle.
Mrs Fairbrother I'm willing.
Mrs Baxter Thank goodness.
Mrs Wells Oh, very well. But there isn't a power point, so there!

Elsie enters R

Mrs Baxter Oh, Elsie, can you plug this in?
Elsie Give it here. There's a point in the hall.

Elsie takes the lead and exits R

Mrs Fairbrother What does it do? Give the birds an electric shock?

Mrs Festoon enters L

Mrs Baxter No, no. Just goes off with a report every so often. Right, Mrs Festoon?
Mrs Festoon That's right. I've set it to work every sixty minutes, see? Then off it goes—bang! Scares the pants off them. It's an hour before they pluck up courage to have another go, and when they do—bang!
Mrs Fairbrother But suppose they come down before the hour is up?
Mrs Festoon They won't. It's scientifically worked out.
Mrs Baxter Sounds perfect.
Mrs Wells It ought to be.
Mrs Festoon What time is it?
Mrs Baxter About four-twenty-five.
Mrs Festoon I've set it to go off at four-thirty, OK?
Mrs Wells Yes. Don't let's waste it, for heaven's sake.
Mrs Baxter (*calling*) Elsie, are you plugged in?

Elsie enters

Elsie I'm plugged in and I'm switched on.
Mrs Baxter Lucky girl. (*To others*) Well, it looks as if our troubles are over.

Elsie That should put paid to your little feathered friends.
Mrs Baxter And the beauty of it is that it doesn't harm them, Mrs
  Fairbrother.
Mrs Fairbrother Did you see the bird we caught, Mrs Festoon?
  (*She moves* L) We put it in this—Oh, it's gone! It must have got
  better and hopped off.
Elsie Never mind, there'll be plenty more soon—nerve cases.
Mrs Festoon I must be off now. Duty calls. (*She crosses to* R)
  Don't worry. You just wait. *Bang!* Cheerio, girls!

Mrs Festoon exits R

Mrs Fairbrother I can't do any more today with my hand.
Mrs Baxter Oh, dear. I had in mind to clean out the ornamental
  pond.

Mrs Wells and Mrs Fairbrother exchange dismayed glances

Mrs Wells Time is marching on, Mrs Baxter.
Mrs Fairbrother And I've a hair appointment.
Mrs Baxter Oh, very well. But please clear up all the equipment.

Mrs Baxter leads Mrs Wells and Mrs Fairbrother; they exit L

Elsie begins to clear the tea things

Lady Cleveland enters R

Elsie What an idea. A bird-scarer. And it cost a packet too.
Lady Cleveland Oh, I can't let them pay for that.
Elsie But they *ordered* the stupid thing.
Lady Cleveland I'm afraid Mrs Baxter gets carried away.
Elsie She'd get carried away if it was up to me.
Lady Cleveland Take comfort, Elsie, there's good news about

Bates. I've just called Mrs Bates and he's home from hospital.
Elsie Oh, madam!
Lady Cleveland Sh! He'll be coming over very shortly to see us.
Elsie Hooray!
Lady Cleveland Sh!
Elsie Why "Sh"?
Lady Cleveland I'm not sure how to break it to the ladies that
  they're not needed anymore. Mrs Baxter could be quite put out.
Elsie Best place for her. Gardeners indeed!
Lady Cleveland It was only a month.
Elsie But what they did in a month!
Lady Cleveland Never mind now. Bates is coming back.
Elsie Yes! Bates is coming back.

They exalt

Mrs Baxter, Mrs Wells and Mrs Fairbrother enter R

Lady Cleveland and Elsie sober up when they see the others enter

Mrs Baxter We'll be off now, Lady Cleveland.
Lady Cleveland I must pay you for the bird-scarer, Mrs Baxter.
Mrs Baxter No, no, we've no intention of that.
Lady Cleveland But I insist. It's my garden after all.
Mrs Baxter But I'm sure you'd never have bought one for
  yourself.
Lady Cleveland Well, I—anyway, I'm sure it will be extremely
  useful and effective.
Mrs Baxter Well, if you're sure. (*She hands over the bill*) Good-
  afternoon, then. See you Thursday. We'll get our own coats,
  Elsie. Goodbye.
Mrs Wells Goodbye.
Mrs Fairbrother Goodbye.

Mrs Baxter, Mrs Wells and Mrs Fairbrother exit R

Lady Cleveland (*looking at the bill and gasping*) Gracious! Oh, well, it was personally crafted.

Elsie You could have had the patch turfed for less.

Lady Cleveland Elsie, is this machine automatic?

Elsie Oh, yes. It should go off any minute now.

Lady Cleveland I mean after that. Does it need winding up or anything?

Elsie Yes. No. I don't know.

Lady Cleveland I'd better go and see if it says anything on it. Call after Mrs Baxter and see if she knows.

Elsie exits R

Lady Cleveland starts towards exit L, *than stops, clapping her hands with delight*

Don't worry, Elsie! Here comes Bates! He's sure to know.

Lady Cleveland exits L

(*Off; calling*) Hallo, Bates! How wonderful to have you back!

Elsie (*off*) Mrs Baxter! Will you come back! Just a minute! We'd like a word with you.

Elsie enters. She is followed by Mrs Baxter, who is putting on her coat

Mrs Baxter What is it, Elsie?

Elsie Lady Cleveland wanted to ask about the bird-scarer. She wants to know about the bang.

Mrs Baxter What about the bang?

Elsie Madam wants to know if it will keep going bang.

Mrs Baxter Well, of course! That's the point, surely.

Elsie But without it having to be re-set or charged-up or anything?

Mrs Baxter Mrs Festoon didn't say anything about it having to be re-set or re-charged. She just said it would keep on going bang. And if Mrs Festoon said it would keep on going bang, Elsie, then I'm perfectly sure it will keep on going bang.

A loud explosion off L

Mrs Wells and Mrs Fairbrother enter R, *running*

Mrs Wells Whatever was that? It was never the bird-scarer.
Mrs Fairbrother It shook the house!
Mrs Baxter It went off! What a marvellous noise! There you are, I told you it would work!
Elsie Lady Cleveland…!
Mrs Baxter Where is she? Tell her we'll have no more trouble with those starlings.
Elsie She was here a moment ago.
Mrs Wells She's not now.
Mrs Fairbrother (*looking* L) She's in the garden. Oh, my goodness!
Elsie Oh, no! What's happened now?

They all hurry to L

Lady Cleveland totters in, dishevelled and with a blackened face, supported by Mrs Willis and Miss Hodge

Elsie helps them move her across to R

Mrs Baxter It worked!
Elsie It certainly did!
Mrs Wells I should hope so. It cost a bomb.
Miss Hodge How appropriate.

Mrs Wells It's knocked the scarecrow for six!

Lady Cleveland Elsie, ring for an ambulance.

Elsie For the scarecrow?

Lady Cleveland It's not the scarecrow—it's Bates! He's flat on his back!

Mrs Willis And you never heard such language!

Elsie Bates!

Lady Cleveland Yes! Oh, Elsie, I think we're back to square one.

Mrs Baxter Never mind, Lady Cleveland, you've still got us.

*The gardeners move towards Lady Cleveland, smiling willingly.
Lady Cleveland takes one look at them and faints*

CURTAIN

FURNITURE AND PROPERTY LIST

On stage: Plants
Settee
2 chairs
Table
Small table
Low table. *On it:* broken pot plant
Trowel

Off stage: Garden fork (**Mrs Fairbrother**)
Pair of clippers (**Mrs Wells**)
Brush and pan (**Elsie**)
Tea things on a tray (**Elsie**)
Scarecrow (**Elsie and Mrs Fairbrother**)
Teapot (**Lady Cleveland**)
Bird (**Mrs Baxter**)
Box (**Elsie**)
Package. *In it:* bird-scarer (**Mrs Festoon**)
Bill (**Mrs Festoon**)

Personal: **Mrs Baxter:** notebook, pen

LIGHTING PLOT

Property fittings requred: nil
Interior. The same scene throughout

To open: Overall general lighting

No cues

EFFECTS PLOT